THE LITTLE BOOK OF
DARUMA DOLLS

BY

PALA WADU MESTHRIGE

Daruma Dolls

Pala Wadu Mesthrige

..... To Pavi and Luna.....

Daruma Dolls

Pala Wadu Mesthrige

DARUMA DOLLS

When you enter Shorinzan Darumaji temple in Japan, you will see a pile of small, egg-like dolls painted in red. Unlike traditional dolls used by kids, which are mostly friendlier in nature, these dolls are scary looking. That's because they have two considerably large eyeballs that stare at you, along with added facial hair. Another interesting feature of the dolls is that they don't have limbs—no arms or legs. Surprisingly, the Japanese use these dolls as a sign of good luck or a good luck charm. But there is more to it.

The tradition of creating and having these dolls dates back many centuries. The legends tell that these dolls were made in remembrance of the monk Bodhidharma, who later went to found Zen Buddhism in China. It is said in the legends that Bodhidharma meditated for nine straight years in search of the ultimate purpose, even though he lost his arms and legs due to not having enough blood flow—the reason Daruma dolls are limbless.

Most temples or vendors in Japan sell these dolls, and within the tradition, there is a particular way of utilizing them.

Daruma Dolls

When you purchase one, you will find they have no pupils in their eyes. You make a wish and color one pupil, usually the left eye. Then, once you fulfill your wish, you color the second or the right pupil and donate it to a temple.

Even more fascinating is that since these dolls are egg-shaped, you can rock them from side to side but they will not fall over. This design reminds us of a profound message—the message of perseverance. When life throws you down, you get up and come back like a Daruma doll.

WHY DID I WANT TO WRITE THIS BOOK?

To this day, there is one phrase quoted by one of my lecturers that has always resonated with me: "Rise through darkness to see the most beautiful sunshine." I had just completed high school when I heard this. It seemed very basic but I didn't fully understand the depth behind this back then. I remember seeing the sports cars driven by the businessmen, for example, but I didn't see the struggles they went through to get them. I thought luck had played a huge part in it. However, it was just a matter of time before I started realizing that my lecturer was right, in almost every case.

I don't intend to write a list of life struggles as an introduction here, as they are very subjective. A particular health issue for one person may not be as severe as for another person. Losing a job while having three kids to feed may not be the same as being single and losing a job. However, I feel deeply for anyone going through any sort of life struggle, and I have lots of respect for anyone who pushes through such obstacles to rise up.

Daruma Dolls

My purpose in writing this book is to give you a different perspective on life struggles and a lesson or two for overcoming them and being resilient. Because, whether you like it or not, struggles in life, from birth to death, are certain, but how you perceive them and move forward is the most important thing.

BE GRATEFUL FOR THE THINGS YOU HAVE IN YOUR LIFE

You may be reading this book while sitting in a comfortable chair, with a roof above your head, and maybe a nice coffee or tea next to you. You may also have your vision, so you can read these letters and process the meaning of these words in your brain. It's not my job to judge your situation, but you likely have had your breakfast, lunch, or dinner today to fill your belly.

Thinking about what you just read, don't you feel so lucky, so fortunate? You have a chair to sit, a roof to shelter yourself, a sip of your favorite drink while reading a book . . .

At the time of writing this, there are almost 900 million people in this world who are going through hunger. That is more than 10 percent of the world's population. More than 150 million people are homeless. And such stats will never end.

Now, forget about the stats for a second. Imagine you are rushing to catch your train, and your foot suddenly hits on a step very hard, and you almost fall on the floor of a busy station.

Daruma Dolls

There is no question about the pain you feel. You may feel embarrassed, frustrated, and disappointed because you just missed your train, as you needed to sit for a while on a bench to feel better before standing up again. While sitting, you see another passenger in a wheelchair trying very hard to get her wheels up to speed so she can reach the lifts and catch her train.

Think about this for a second. You feel frustrated, as you just missed the train because you had to rest a bit after you hit a stair. If you are a regular commuter, what are the chances this could happen? But how about the routine for the lady in a wheelchair? Every day she has to make an extra effort to get to the station and onto the train. While most modern facilities have disabled access, frankly, the luxury you had of being able to quickly run through the stairs and catch the train was not available for the lady in the wheelchair. How lucky you are!

I think there is a reason why our parents, teachers, preachers, and religious leaders asked and taught us to practice gratitude and be thankful for what we have: because we are lucky. We are very fortunate to have food on the table, a nice pair of shoes, books to read and pencils to write, a mattress or bed to sleep on, a phone with a camera to click a picture and upload it on Instagram. But how often do we really *feel* fortunate?

How often do we practice giving gratitude for what we have? Thinking of all the good things we have in our lives only takes a few seconds.

However, most of us only think about what we don't like about our lives. But how tough do you really have it? Maybe you wake up and feel that you can't go to work because your job is hard for the salary you are offered by your employer. Your neighbor, on the other hand, just had a pay cut or his hours cut, as his employer had to operate with Covid restrictions. Plus, you just got a call from one of your closest friends, saying she lost her job altogether. Needless to say, when only minutes ago you thought your job was hard, whining about the salary you receive for what you do, just by comparing others' situations, you suddenly feel the luxury of having a job in the first place and being able to feed the family.

When life feels tough, we merely need to think of all we have compared to those less fortunate than us and feel gratitude for those things, however small they may seem. When you practice gratitude, it helps reduce your stress and pain levels. It improves the cognitive function of the area of the brain and neural network that is the same area that ignites when we socialize and feel pleasure. Being grateful as a practice is one of the best exercises a depressed person can perform.

When you simply are grateful for the things you have in your life, your whole mindset becomes positive, focused on the good instead of the bad. This practice is so powerful that not only does it suppress negative emotions, but it enhances positive feelings.

Take media mogul Oprah as an example. We all know that she did not have a comfortable life growing up. Toughness was a part of her life until she became a star. However, she is one of the celebrities who practices gratitude every day. In an interview, she once was asked to show her gratitude journal. She had noted, "Eating cold melon on a bench in the sun," such a small thing for a celebrity like her to be grateful for. She truly believes that such a practice helped her become who she is despite her past struggles in life.

"But what if I am a crazy-busy person who doesn't even have a second to be mindful about my morning coffee?" you may ask. To that I would say, there is a person who has changed thousands if not millions of lives of ordinary people and directed numerous businesses to success. People pay premiums to get seats at his coaching sessions, as his time and motivational power are gold. Once struggling in life, he now uses his private jet for work to save time on travel. This man, Tony Robbins, is that busy trying to enhance the lives of others.

Yes, he is blessed, and he practices gratitude every day regardless of his schedule. He believes being grateful for the simple things in life will allow you to focus on the positives in life and dump fear and anger.

Now, contrary to what you may have seen others do, you don't need to maintain a journal or have a gratitude buddy or post on your Twitter to show your gratitude. All you need is to take a second or two to appreciate a simple thing in your life and feel how lucky you are at the present moment.

Studies show that people who practice gratitude, even those who have tough lives, will experience less stress and depression, have increased positivity, and, most importantly, feel a high possibility of attaining their goals in the future, which I think is the foundation for overcoming a difficult life.

Daruma Dolls

PERSISTENCE BEATS RESISTANCE

We all know how a toddler gets grumpy and starts making drama in a shopping center when he isn't allowed to buy a toy he wants. However, in the end, most parents end up buying the toy. Think about this for a second. The boy knows that he wants the toy badly. That's his vision. He asks his parents to get it for him with hope planted in his mind. The moment he is refused the toy, he, in turn, refuses to give up on what he envisioned. The course of action is the most interesting part here. That is to keep crying, yelling, rolling on the floor, and creating all sorts of drama until the parents agree to buy the toy. The boy is persistent in troubling his parents, continuously pushing to show that he badly wants the toy no matter what his parents think. Some children always win with this tactic of being persistent in asking for what they want or refusing what they don't like.

Joanne's mother passed away tragically, and she went into deep depression. She flew to a different country to forget all these negatives and start a new life.

Even though she found her temporary love as an English teacher, she had to go through a tough divorce, ending up as a single parent to a beautiful daughter. She came back to Scotland and was surviving on government support. Now more depressed, yet determined, she restarted the writing of her novel. With full hope, she sent her manuscript to twelve publishers seeking a book deal, only to get rejection after rejection. Then one day, thanks to the eight-year-old daughter of another publisher, her first novel was published. The rest was history.

Joanne Kathleen Rowling is said to be richer than her Majesty the Queen, and the Harry Potter franchise doesn't require an introduction. Thanks to her perseverance, part of history has been written magically. Though she temporarily gave up writing after her mother passed away, there was a tiny little bit of persistence in her to continue her writing even after her divorce. Perhaps all these struggles fueled her to push herself. It's not uncommon for early writers to be rejected numerous times by publishers, but it's the lucky next submission that can make you a star or a millionaire.

Harland Davis Sanders's story is similar. Before he became the face of the famous franchise chain KFC, his secret chicken recipe was rejected more than one thousand times by potential buyers. Only his perseverance to keep believing in his creation when others didn't made him a success.

Daruma Dolls

Persistence is a sustained effort carried out through a tough time, as you believe that's the only way forward. Sometimes persistence is used by a person as a tool of internal retaliation for a challenge posed by external sources. While Sanders believed in his recipe, part of him wanted to prove that other restaurants were mistaken to turn his recipe down. He was persistent in finding the perfect buyer to prove that it was the ultimate chicken recipe.

Sometimes perseverance is sticking to a plan. It is a course of action you take within a given period of time, repetitively.

Think about a person whose weight is more than four hundred pounds. His physical body doesn't allow him to freely do what an average weighted person does. Relatively, he struggles with his daily work, and life seems hard and challenging. He decides to shed some calories, to eat less and work out every day for at least thirty minutes until he reaches his goal of three hundred pounds and then two hundred pounds, and so on.

This is an example of persistence being not willpower but a method—a set of actions built into our daily routine to accomplish something. It is like brushing our teeth every day. You don't need to push yourself consciously; it's more like an activity to check off your checklist.

The best thing about a simple routine or plan is that after some time, it can become a habit, as it said that after about sixty-six days of doing something, it becomes a part of your life.

Take the world's number one male tennis player in the world, Djokovic, as an example. He knows that the final could go for hours, unlike a typical tennis game, especially if he meets an opponent like Federer who is as good as him. To be on the court, playing his best game for extended hours, how many hours per day do you think he has to practice? He has a plan. He has a routine to follow so that he is sure he is fit for the day.

Persistence is easy when you ignore the noise around you. It's where you omit your distractions and laser focus on what needs to be done. This noise can sometimes be your own inner voice or external factors. For example, if you want to eat healthily all the time, the inner noise will distract you by reminding you how good a burger tastes. Another example would be if you want to earn that promotion badly. Inner noises like, "I might not be qualified for the job," or external noises coming from a co-worker like, "No one has ever survived more than three months in this role," need to be ignored. Instead, in these cases, you should only focus on eating healthily and getting that promotion.

PERSISTENCE BEATS MEDIOCRITY

Persistence applies to both smart cookies and average cookies. What I mean here is that whether you are smart, have talent, or are regarded as gifted or not, if you keep practicing persistence, you can overcome your struggles.

Suppose an artist who has just finished her one-of-a-kind canvas painting is about to sell it at an upcoming auction for a hefty price. The day before, a fire breaks out at her studio and destroys her piece. Obviously, she is shattered, feeling her whole world is ending. However, she is talented. If she is determined to rebuild the same piece or one similar, all she has to do is be persistent and continue on her journey to come up with another million-dollar art piece.

What if you are not talented enough or smart enough (or you think you are not) to overcome your struggles through persistence? The answer is simple: be persistent. What if you are broke? No one is there to help you out financially, you don't have any belongings other than a laptop, and you'd love to make a living out of being a programmer or a coder, but you don't know anything about coding.

Dr. Carol Dweck, in her book *Mindset*, talks about the very same concept: having mediocre talent and a growth mindset and being persistent. With hundreds if not thousands of real-life examples, she would tell the young person above to have a growth mindset and be persistent in learning to code. Now, if you have mediocre talent, you can't be an overnight success, but you can still be successful.

PRACTICE HANSEI

The Japanese teach and practice a concept called *hansei*, which can be translated as "self-reflection." It means acknowledging your mistakes and making improvements. Sometimes it is regarded as a pledge for improvement. This is very powerful because the mistakes we have made in the past are just that, in the past. They cannot be changed. But having a commitment to working on improvements with a growth mindset helps overcome life struggles.

ENJOY SMALL WINS

We celebrate things like birthdays, wedding anniversaries, business start-ups, publishing a book, etc. Often, these events are pretty significant milestones in our lives that are worth having a glass of champagne for. But what about a person going through bad times, going through chemo treatments, or having only a small amount in his bank account? What are the chances he would celebrate his birthday with a happy face?

There are millions of borrowers in the United States who are swamped with a huge debt burden. For some, it is a matter of time before they go bankrupt and lose everything. Among these, there are determined people who are trying really hard to pay off their debt and come out of the dark tunnel they are in. If you know the concept of *debt snowballing*, every time you pay off your smallest debt, I think you should drink to that. You may owe $700,000 to your bank, but if you pay off your credit card of $5,000, you should celebrate that. It's a small win!

When you enjoy small wins, whether it's a glass of champagne or time off from your office, it creates a trigger within you that you have achieved something and are now reaping a benefit.

Daruma Dolls

Our brain is structured in such a way that it will then seek to have the next celebration. It automatically pushes us to the next course of action so it can enjoy the next glass of champagne. This time it can be a nice dinner, or a getaway when you pay off your car loan. This will continue to motivate you to stay the course until you get to the end goal, despite your struggles, or despite how much debt you still have. It's irrelevant what your next debt payoff is. It could be your home mortgage you owe $500,000 on, but your brain will start to think this is doable, as you have done similar things in the past.

You will also be motivated by your perceived progression in life. Think about the initial life of an entrepreneur who has just started a clothing line. It's a huge challenge to compete with the existing brands, be profitable, and be sustainable. Surely there are mini goals or targets to be achieved before becoming a well-known brand in the market. But when you get that first few thousand dollars for the funding from VCs who believe in your proposal and when you recognize this small win and celebrate, this gets ticked off as progress made toward becoming a world-class clothing retailer. The same goes for the next steps, when you find the right designers and pattern makers, the ideal suppliers and plant, the best marketers, the perfect buyers, and the list goes on. Looking back, connecting the dots, and recognizing these small steps will give you a sense of achievement despite all your challenges.

This will boost your level of confidence as well. You clearly know that you have made progress through dark times, and when you encounter the next challenge, you will have the inner assurance to move forward and conquer it.

Indirectly, celebrating small wins makes us accountable for our end goal. It gives us some sort of responsibility. When the clothing designer celebrates selling her first one thousand pieces of clothing, she knows she is in the game. Her loyal employees are looking for the next paycheck, investors are expecting a decent return, and the charity getting 50 cents from every top she sells is counting on her. These future accountabilities create more determination, more committed plans.

Daruma Dolls

KNOW THE WORST-CASE SCENARIO

When Colonel Sanders went from buyer to buyer with the hope of selling his secret recipe, he had two potential outcomes: the buyer would invest, or the buyer would say no. Every instance when he stepped into a meeting with a potential buyer, he knew the worst outcome would have been them saying no. What does it feel like to know the worst case?

Knowing the worst case that could happen enables us to prepare ourselves in advance—especially mentally. Having it happen would never be a curve ball to us, as we already know it may be coming. By knowing the worst case, we ensure there are no surprises. We know that the smallest favorable result that happens above that level is a positive result.

Using this method should give you peace of mind, so you can stop worrying and start finding solutions.

Dave Ramsey has gone bankrupt not only once but twice. If you read his materials and listen to his podcasts, you know he knows what it is like to hit rock bottom.

He has experienced the worst that could happen financially, but he came back stronger and better. Knowing that it's the worst that could happen and that you made it out the other side only makes you stronger if you don't let it hold you down.

Knowing and expecting the worst case are two different things. What I mean here is to know it, not to expect it. Expecting is similar to manifesting. This is where you keep thinking about the worst case and you plant it inside your subconscious so it becomes true in your life. That's wrong. Constantly thinking about the worst is like telling the universe that you want it. What you want to do instead is know the worst case but look forward to having all the positives beyond it, which is what you really want.

When Navy Seal Jason Redman was shot multiple times during an ambush in Iraq and regained consciousness on the hospital bed, he came to the realization that the worst had happened to him. Doctors said that his limbs were of no use, and his face was partially destroyed by bullets, but he didn't give up. He saw this as point X, the worst point he could be at, and knew that any step out of this zone was growth and what he needed to work toward. He went on to become one of the most famous and respected life coaches in the world and now helps people fight against life struggles and find forward momentum.

Daruma Dolls

Another major benefit of knowing and accepting the worst case is that it allows us to understand the reality—what has actually happened or the present situation. Sometimes it could be future state as well. Reality is something that cannot be denied, no matter how hard you try to deceive your mind. The $20,000 you just lost in the poker machine, the flash flood that took your livestock, your employer going bankrupt, and you losing your job—these types of things are all reality, and you cannot change them.

Back in Lord Buddha's days, a lady named Kisa visited Buddha's monastery, trying to find a solution for the unfortunate events that had just happened in her life. Her husband had been killed by an army, leaving her with two children. While crossing a river, one of her kids was swept away by the water current while her other child was taken off by an eagle. Devastated and full of sorrow, she knew the worst had happened to her. As she sought a solution to her problem from Buddha, Buddha ordered her to go and find a handful of mustard seeds from a household whose close or distant family member hadn't died. She spent days searching for these mustard seeds with the hope of finding a solution, but she eventually came to the realization that death is common for everyone and was not a problem faced only by herself. She was shown the worst case, losing all her loved ones, and she learned the lesson of accepting reality.

She knew that she could not do anything to bring her husband and children back to life. She then became a monk and found her pathway to attain Nibbana, which is enlightenment in Buddhism.

Worst cases always present us with options. When Dave Ramsey hit rock bottom, he had options. The options were to remain broke or find a way out of his financial struggles. Jason Redman knew he had been wounded badly when he woke up in the hospital bed. His options were to give up and remain paralyzed and hide his face from the world or to bounce back and walk again. Steve Jobs had the option to give up on his creation, Apple, or to come back and fight for his leadership position when he was thrown out of CEO-ship. When Kisa's whole family died, she had the option of continuing to deny it and suffer, or she could learn to face the reality and live past her pain.

You also have the option to give up or to accept reality and be mentally strong. Thinking about the adversity doesn't do any good. You have to learn to bounce back from it and move forward with your life. So many people have done it. You can do it too. Figure out the worst case, realize you don't have to live in fear of it happening to you, and find solutions to achieve your dreams.

REALIZE IT'S NOT JUST YOU

Your adversity may seem unique. You may feel that such things only happen to you. If you have just failed an exam by two points, you may feel, "Why only me?" If you have not been granted a visa to enter a country you want to migrate to, you may feel, "Why me?" If you have just lost your child, you may feel, "Why me?" While it may seem very personal at the beginning, if you put some thought into it, you must understand that your adversity is not merely unique to you. It happens to others too. The world has nearly eight billion people. Once you understand this fact, it is easier to understand the reality and come out of the challenges. This will open your eyes, just like Kisa's eyes were opened when Buddha demonstrated that she was not the only person in the world who had lost loved ones.

Pala Wadu Mesthrige

THERE IS NO SUCH THING AS FAILURE, ONLY LEARNING

When you promised your business partner you would bring enough investors to lift up your dying company and you did not, you failed. When you are unemployed and just received a phone call from a recent interview telling you there were better candidates, you failed. It is tough to go through failures. Many people ask, what's the use of all the time, energy, and money spent only to fail in the end? However, the golden question you should be asking is, "Did I actually fail?"

When Space-X could not land their returning rockets on the landing ships successfully after months of testing, attempt after attempt, Elon Musk was under enormous pressure from every angle. Critics had already called it impossible, and everyone expected Space-X to be a failure. Musk and his company have now proven that the concept of the reusable launch system is no longer a fantasy.

You may have heard that Michael Jordan was cut from his high school basketball team. He was probably devastated about it back then.

Daruma Dolls

And how about missing the game-winning shot on twenty-six occasions, especially after becoming a star? Those were failures—big fat failures. He has failed over and over again in his career, and that's how he became the Jordan we know.

Failures give us an opportunity—an opportunity to know why and where we failed. If we look at them objectively in order to learn and grow, we will see our failures can tell us what went wrong and how we can do better next time. Space-X uses data from its failed attempts to analyze why their rockets did not land safely on the pad. Jordan likely analyzed his elbows, release point, follow-through, or maybe even mental focus to figure out why those shots didn't go in. For the above job applicant, she may realize that the lack of research she did about the prospective company cost her the job, so next time she will do her research.

Pala Wadu Mesthrige

PRACTICE NANA KOROBI YA OKI

The country of Japan has experienced disaster after disaster. It has stood through a great earthquake in 1923, nuclear bombs at Hiroshima and Nagasaki in 1945, the Kobe earthquake in 1955, and recently, a tsunami and nuclear meltdowns, just to name a few. But what is most interesting to see is the turnaround of the country as a whole. After all the setbacks, the comeback was stronger than ever before, by everyone. If you use social media, you likely have seen how quickly Japan rebuilt what it lost, within a shorter period of time, and is now better and stronger.

"Fall down seven times, stand up eight," is the general idea behind, "Nana karobi ya oki." This phrase of resilience is built into the culture of Japanese people. In my opinion, this is not just a reminder to get up at your first failure, but what will likely be many failures through your journey. Your next try could be a win, so get up and try again. If you had a chance to go speak to locals about the natural disasters they experienced, this phrase, "Nana karobi ya oki," would commonly be heard among them. The attitude is inbuilt in the Japanese culture.

Daruma Dolls

Daruma dolls embody the saying, "Nana karobi ya oki." It doesn't matter which direction you push the doll, due to its heavy bottom—or in human terms, due to perseverance—it comes back up.

DRINK TO THAT FAILURE

Failure is something that happens in hindsight. Unless your motives are evil, you cannot simply plan for failure. It's a result you just look back at, something that has happened in the past. While humans celebrate good things that happened in the past, can you celebrate failures?

I'm not sure whether Edison drank a glass of champagne for every one of his purported ten thousand failed attempts at commercializing the light bulb. But the point is, the point at which you realize you have failed is a victory you need to acknowledge and celebrate. You need to realize that you gave your full effort and learned something, even though you didn't get the end result you wanted. In Edison's case, each of the ten thousand times he learned not to make the lightbulb a commercial success was an opportunity to move on to the next experiment. When you miss a tight deadline to deliver a sales report to your supervisor, it is a failure, but if you learn a lesson and understand why it happened, just have a glass of wine for that. Next time you'll know what to do.

Daruma Dolls

The same concept goes for breakup parties. Say you have just gone through a tough breakup after ending a ten-year relationship with your partner and you feel like a failure. Celebrating this moment will send you positive vibes, and most importantly, it's a celebration of your learning. You have learned what you can bring to the next relationship to make it work.

DARE TO FAIL GREATLY

Going through tough times sometimes requires you to take the next level of risk, push yourself to an unknown territory, and take an action you have never taken before. Think about an entrepreneur who is on the edge of bankruptcy but knows that the only way out is to put his new product on the market. It's a huge risk in terms of the money he may have invested, his reputation, his valuable time and relationships, etc.

Elon Musk was on the verge of giving up hope for his company, having faced hard times from investors, critics, and employees and having gone bankrupt. But he knew that his vision had something this world could benefit from. He took a great risk to achieve his dream. He ended up putting up his own private money to save the company, and the rest became history.

Going through tough times may tempt you to take any kind of risk. But here, you have to be a little cautious, because you don't want to put yourself further down from where you are. Suppose you only have a few thousand dollars to live on. You wouldn't just go place a bet on horses or a poker machine, right?

Daruma Dolls

That would be a misuse of the money you have. So it's not about taking risks blindly. It's about having a plan and a strategy. Musk knew that he had only his private money to save the company, and he invested it, but he had a plan and strategy for doing so.

DON'T BE EMBARRASSED ABOUT THE FAILURES

Embarrassment is either externally focused or internally focused. If you are trying hard to lose weight but because of a health issue you can't shed the pounds as expected, and you think your friends will laugh at you secretly, then this feeling is externally driven. If you are trying hard to be good at public speaking, yet your speeches are not up to your expectations, then you may feel embarrassed about yourself. This is internally driven.

Whether it's internally or externally driven, embarrassment doesn't last long. It's temporary. But it's admittable that you may feel this even for a second. That's human nature. If you have the will and hope and keep pushing through your failures, this temporary feeling of embarrassment will be a thing of the past.

Why do you think people like celebrities and businesspeople go on podiums and talk about their mistakes in public? If they were embarrassed about their mistakes, would they share their stories with us?

Daruma Dolls

The point is that the learning must be substituted with embarrassment. If and when you feel embarrassed after a failure, always try to think about the bright side. Ask yourself, "What have I learned from that?"

Being afraid of embarrassment will only let you down. It will stop you from taking the next step or finding the solution to your problem.

When Covid hit hard back in 2020, the travel industry was affected greatly, if not the worst of all industries. Pilots lost their jobs as flights were grounded. Most pilots had to live on government support. Due to these hard times, some pilots started working in other industries. Some have become cafe wait staff or delivery or courier drivers. Here, it is not to say that one job is better than the other. But imagine being a pilot who worked many years and had to become part of the wait staff for his neighborhood coffee shop. Forget about the earlier mentioned externally driven embarrassment, but how would they feel internally? Either way, these pilots pushed really hard through difficult times. They knew the embarrassment they may have felt was temporary and just a mere feeling.

STEP OUT OF YOUR COMFORT ZONE

It's uncomfortable for anyone to change their existing zone of operation. This is the zone you feel comfortable and relaxed in, as you know the ins and outs of it. But what if you are challenged or threatened by an external source that requires you to step outside your comfort zone? This will be difficult for you, for starters, and it could be intimidating as well.

Think about the life of a migrant who leaves for another country seeking a better standard of living. She may have had a well-recognized, well-paid job back in her country. She may have had properties, vehicles, friends, and family. But when migrating to another country and leaving all this behind, she is not guaranteed to have the same things. She is stepping out of her comfort zone to take advantage of opportunities like a better life and future. This is challenging and intimidating, as it is unknown territory.

Suppose you have been a production manager in your company for the last ten-plus years. You know every detail about the production, from design to distribution.

Daruma Dolls

Suddenly your plant is relocated overseas due to cost concerns, and you have been told by the management that one option for remaining with the company is joining the marketing department. You know nothing about marketing, so this is unknown territory. You feel that life would be hard, no longer comfortable, and possibly tough.

The question you may be asking is, "Why would the immigrant woman in the example above leave her country in the first place?" The answer is, for the potential for a better life, opportunities she didn't have back in her country—maybe a better job, better health care, a friendlier community, cleaner air. For the ex-production manager, the choice to leave his comfort zone is not his, but it could be an opportunity to upskill in another area, get a better pay package, get a new and exciting job role, and meet new stakeholders.

So, stepping out of your comfort zone could be voluntary or forced. The migrant chose to step outside, whereas the production manager was forced by external circumstances. Life will present both of these situations to you. Either way, the new zone can feel intimidating and challenging at first. But what you need to focus on is the positive things the new zone can bring you.

Richard Branson admits that he doesn't enjoy public speaking. Every time he is in front of an audience, it is outside his comfort zone.

But he mastered it anyway, as this skill is a must for him being the face of his Virgin brand.

Jim Carey, a great comedian, once tested his boundaries by taking a role as Joel in Michael Gondry's film *Eternal Sunshine of the Spotless Mind*. This proved to him and the world that not only is he great in comedies but also in dramas/sci-fis.

Stepping outside your comfort zone will prepare you to face future challenges as well. You know you did it in the past, so you are not afraid to take risks.

KNOW YOUR WHY

Think about the life of a diamond miner in Sierra Leone. Every day he wakes up, works under hard conditions, and takes minimal toilet breaks to earn a few dollars. He does this because he wants to feed his family, afford an education for his children, and maybe get medicine for his ill mom. Maybe one day he wants to be the boss of the mine.

Human beings have a purpose for anything they do in their life. There is a component of *why* in our life. Take a moment and think about any action you take. Whether it's good or bad, each action has its own why. Except for when we are unconscious, the only time we don't know our purposes is when we are infants. Infants don't have a purpose in this regard, only acting according to their biological needs. They wake up, sleep, and eat when their body tells them to. The capacity to establish a purpose at this age is absent. In contrast to an infant, if you can read this book, you should have some sort of purpose in your life.

An athlete who trains for a marathon runs miles and miles, rain or shine, because she wants to win the gold medal.

That is her purpose. A battalion starves in the jungle for two days while they keep an eye on the enemy so they can attack at the right time. That's their purpose. A cancer patient adheres to all treatments despite their struggles because their purpose is to defeat the illness.

Viktor Frankl survived three years in Auschwitz. It's unnecessary to tell the details of life in a Nazi concentration camp back in the 1950s—but was the worst. So how did he survive despite all these adversities? He had a purpose and why for being alive. He had a reason to live, a reason to ignore all these horrible things happening inside the camp.

Prior to being imprisoned by the Nazis, Frankl was a psychologist and was working on writing a book. He took this manuscript to the camp when he was captured, but unfortunately, the soldiers destroyed it. Viktor had heavily invested his time and effort into writing this book, which was his mission. This was one of the main things that kept him alive throughout his difficult times inside the camp. He knew that the work of writing his book, something that only he could fulfill, was his why for living. The hope that he would one day go out and publish his book gave him the strength to live.

In his book, *Man's Search for Meaning*, he talks about having a why or purpose in life.

Daruma Dolls

He saw that the prisoners of the concentration camp who had a reason to live lived longer, and many of them survived. Some people's reason was to see their loved ones again. Some had unfinished projects they wanted to complete. These were their whys for living, and they got out of the camp. Viktor explains that most of the inmates died not merely due to deteriorated physical conditions but also because they had no reason to live. They lost hope. Such inmates got sick frequently and badly and gave up on life too soon.

Purpose is a destination we try to go to. It's why we do things. It's the ultimate goal we try to achieve. It's the hope. Yet your purpose doesn't always come on a silver platter. Often, external factors and events happen in our lives, especially negative ones, and it may seem those factors or events affect our purpose and push us away from our vision, but we shouldn't let this happen.

It's similar to when we color one eye of Daruma initially. By doing this, we establish a purpose, a goal, and hope. We tell ourselves that whatever obstacles come our way, we only focus on achieving our mission by overcoming our struggles.

That miner may or may not have shoes or slippers to wear while working. He probably doesn't have a roof over him, a raincoat, or appropriate safety gear. He may not get sick leave like a typical office worker.

He probably has to work fourteen-plus hours, day and night, to earn those few dollars. These are external conditions, hard factors that present when you try to achieve your goal, roadblocks that threaten you when you try to get closer to your *why*.

While we can challenge some externalities, others challenge us. If you are going through a horrible personal relationship with your partner, you have the option to move out. If public speaking is a great fear for you, but you have to do it to win your next proposal, then you can go and work on those skills. If you have a lower-paying job, you can either change your job or get an extra part-time delivery job to earn some extra money. All these types of externalities present you with an option. However, there are other externalities that hinder your journey to your purpose that can't be changed. A loving wife who just lost her husband can't bring him back from the dead. If your doctor says that the only option to save your life is to amputate your limb, then you must face this.

Life is full of externalities. Regardless of whether they can be changed or not, this is the reality, past, present, and future. Nothing stays the way we want in our life. That's the truth. Let's say your mission is to be the best organic potato chip manufacturer in your country.

Daruma Dolls

As you work toward this, you will be challenged by intense competition, regulatory pressure, funding and shareholder issues, customer complaints, bad media, and potato diseases. These are all things you cannot change. They are your reality, things you cannot have the way you want, as life is just unfair sometimes.

As another example, say you have been selected for the final interview for your dream job, but the day before the interview, you catch the flu and cannot get out of bed. This is reality, and you cannot change it. However, once you understand this concept of reality, your eyes will be open, and you will have a context to think around. You will realize that though situations out of our control may occur, we still have control over ourselves and how we react to and handle the situation.

If you are constantly criticized or not supported by your team members at your company, you may feel sad, angry, and disappointed. This is a fact, a reality. You may not be able to change the behavior and thoughts of your team members toward you, but you cannot let your sadness, anger, and disappointment crush your goals either. Instead of getting drowned by these feelings and harming your end goal, you can seek options as solutions to overcome this issue.

Perhaps it could be a friendly help-seeking conversation with your peers or supervisor to see how you can learn from your mistakes, or perhaps it could be to leave the team or organization as the final option to reach your highest career goal.

If you have just gone through a divorce, that is the reality. You cannot change it. You cannot let the feeling of sadness, emptiness, loneliness, or disappointment overtake your life. The only way out of these externalities is how you respond to them, how you change your attitude and behavior toward these issues. You have to stay the course, seek options, and simply move forward.

HANDLE ADVERSITY THE RIGHT WAY

When we are going through difficult times, we tend to make both positive and negative decisions. These actions will either help us recover, get out of the position, and move forward, or will keep us in the same position if not worse. We don't need to worry about the positive decisions, as they are the right ones, but what about the negative decisions we make, both physical and mental?

Suppose you are going through a breakup that hit hard, and to forget the thoughts around that, you start sipping whiskey, which then becomes an alcohol addiction. This harms your body. Excessive smoking and taking drugs to forget a scenario have the same effect. You are making a harmful or negative decision for your physical health. On the other hand, if you are constantly thinking about your recently lost loved one or blaming yourself constantly for the money you have lost gambling, these are also negative, affecting our mental health.

If you do this, you are not alone. Most humans make some negative decisions after an adverse situation has occurred, even if just for a short time.

But what we need to really think about is whether these decisions help us in the long run or not—are they helping us or harming us? I am not suggesting here that you shouldn't mourn when you lose your loved one. But you can't keep thinking about it continuously for a long period. This won't bring your loved one back, nor does it help you focus on and progress in your daily life. The sorrow, pain, emptiness, or even anger doesn't lift you up from where you are. It may take a while for you to understand this concept, but it will really help you bounce back.

ACHIEVEMENTS DO NOT HAPPEN OVERNIGHT

Passing an exam, winning that gold medal, and getting the new job you have recently applied for are all achievements. On the other hand, overcoming adversity is also an achievement. Ending a toxic relationship, putting a stop to grieving your recently passed mom, or even the very first step of thinking you will come out of any adversity is an achievement in itself.

The point of identifying and recognizing the achievement is an interesting subject. Because society and even we as individuals have the habit of thinking that the achievement happens overnight or at a particular point in time.

When the Harry Potter series, whether we're talking about the set of books or the movie franchise, started to catch on and became the novel or movie of the year, it seemed Rowling had hit the jackpot—a quick, big win. But while it was the jackpot for her, it definitely was not an overnight success.

As it's commonly known, it is the things that are beneath the iceberg—the loneliness, tears, half-filled stomach, four hours of sleep, two shirts for the entire week, and many other things—that are the pillars for "overnight" success. These are the things others don't see, things going on behind the backstage. For you to put on a good show one day, you have to have this foundation poured correctly.

NOW IS THE RIGHT TIME

When you are going through tough times, you might feel that you want to wait a few days, weeks, or even years to start over. You may not be confident, or you may have doubts in the present. You may try to establish a false assumption of a time frame in the future, saying, "I will do X after Y date to overcome Z." But how do you know when it is the right time to move forward from your struggles? It's like waiting until economic conditions are in your favor to start your business, or waiting until all your financial problems are over to get married to your partner. How do you know that ending your financial problems will necessarily end other life challenges? What if your inner self again says to wait another few months or years until you get your career problems sorted? You see, there is no perfect time to wait for. Don't wait for the auspicious moment. If it comes, it won't last forever. It's not worth delaying your life for. Stop worrying about your troubles and start finding a way out of them. As they say, the best time to start a business is during hard times.

Similar to the above is trying to put an age around your adversities.

Suppose you are in your late forties and struggling professionally, as you don't have the necessary qualifications. Others are climbing the ladder, and you have been stuck at the same pay grade for the last fifteen years. What is stopping you from pursuing the degree or certificate you want? Suppose you went through an ugly divorce in your fifties, and for the last few years you have been alone. What is stopping you from going out and finding your next Mr. or Mrs.? You see, age is just a number. You are never late to the party.

IT'S OKAY TO ASK FOR HELP

One day during the Covid pandemic, I was scrolling through my Facebook news feed, and suddenly a post from a local group caught my eye. A single mom said she was struggling and needed help in terms of groceries and baby items. The post had been up for about fifteen to thirty minutes, and you should have seen the love poured from other people in the comments. People were asking for her address so they could drop goodies at the door. Some people had keyed in kind words to lift her mood. Some babysitters offered their service free of charge for a couple of hours to take care of the infant she had. It was so satisfying to see such help come from the community.

You see, the world is not as cruel as we think. There are beautiful people out there, generous and kind people. It's not only the philanthropists who do good for the world. Average people are willing to help others too. When difficult times hit you, all you need to do is go the extra step of asking for help. It might be a little difficult, intimidating, and uncomfortable to do, as you may have feelings like shame and shyness, but these kind people won't judge your circumstances.

EVERYTHING CHANGES EVENTUALLY

The only constant thing in the world is change. That's the ultimate universal truth. Good times and bad times alike will come and go. The secret is to embrace your adversities and hard times and face them head-on. In that way, your times of trial will be shorter.

If you have ever tried to find a job, perhaps you failed interview after interview, and it felt like you were having a hard time. But once you secured a job, how did you feel about that experience or time? It was definitely a thing of the past, right? Maybe you went through a complicated surgery that created mental stress within your family. But once you were fully recovered, you were all happy and back to normal. The stressful time was a thing of the past. The same goes for if you didn't have a penny to buy a loaf of bread a few years ago but now you live a comfortable life. Your problems have changed now.

All these adversities are temporary stops in our lives. You may feel like it lasted months or years, and in some cases maybe it did, but it is a much shorter period compared to your whole life, when you reflect back. Our bad times always pass.

Daruma Dolls

You only realize how short they actually were when you look back and connect the dots. I'm sure you've heard someone say, "Everything will be all right." That is exactly right. Time changes everything. For a positive and determined mind, adversities are just like temporary dark clouds in the sky where the sun comes next to bring you the sunshine. So keep your chin up and move forward.

A LITTLE UNCERTAINTY AND STRESS ARE GOOD

Think back to your school or university days. You had a goal of getting through your exams and achieving a good grade or passing a class. Additionally, you may have had to live up to the expectations of your parents, teacher, or partner. Getting your degree, getting better grades, or passing a certain class also might have had some potential impact on your future job. Simply put, better results would equal a better job. You may have paid some money toward your exams or gotten a loan for it from the government. Therefore the only option was to get through your exams. All of this may have caused some stress or fear around the thought, "What if I fail?"

While stress is usually given a negative connotation, having a little stress and uncertainty helps you prepare for unknowns. In this case you would create a plan to study hard, do revisions and mock papers, and try to be efficient with the time and resources you have.

Daruma Dolls

It's the same when you have back-to-back requirements from your boss at your office. You tend to find ways to get things done by being efficient and thinking outside the box.

The same goes for when you want to find some money for the sudden ill your father has faced. The stress causes you to talk to your close relatives, do some extra hours at work, and be creative and start a side gig to get that extra money.

Studies done by the University of Berkeley on rats found that significant but brief stressful events caused stem cells in their brains to proliferate into new nerve cells that, when mature two weeks later, improved the rats' mental performance (https://news.berkeley.edu,2013).

Challenges are never ending in our life, and stress is an inherent part of it. However, the right kind and level of stress makes you a tough cookie. As you overcome challenges, you gain confidence that you can do it again in the future during uncertain times.

LEVERAGE THE VALUE OF OPPORTUNITY VS. OBLIGATION

This topic is purely a mind game. Basically it's how you think, your perception. To explain this concept, let me give you an example. Let's say you are overweight. I want you to think about all the struggles you are facing daily: not being able to wear your favorite dress or shirt, not being able to freely eat what you crave, having to take medication prescribed by your doctor, or even having trouble getting into your own car, etc. Now, what is your opportunity here? The opportunity is to reduce your weight and get in shape. However, your obligation is to eat homemade meals, give up ice cream, hit the gym daily, take the stairs, cut down on alcohol, etc. Here is the kicker: If you keep focusing on your *obligation* and treating it as a burden, then you will not tap into your *opportunity*. Instead, you only want to think about achieving your opportunity. This is your ultimate goal. Your mind could still ask you not to hit the gym or eat that burger, but you really need to delay your instant gratification for your opportunity.

Take another example. Let's say you are not doing well financially or are poor. Your opportunity is to become wealthy so you can have a comfortable life.

Daruma Dolls

And what is your obligation? It is to stop partying every weekend and buying the upgraded version of your smartphone every time it comes out, automate your savings, cut down your holiday travel, etc. This is all instant gratification. As mentioned above, it's always better to focus on your opportunity here than to see your obligation as a burden.

Simply put, whatever issue you have, picture your opportunity here and make obligation your plan. Focus only on your opportunity while letting the obligation to do its work.

HAVE EMPATHY TOWARD OTHERS

Let's think about this for a moment. Suppose during Covid, you lost your job, the only income stream you and your family had. This was a very hard time. You struggled to put food on the table and had to go to the food pantry of a local charity to get free food.

Fast-forward a couple of years, and suppose you are doing well. You drive past the same charity and happen to notice a few people standing in line at the same food pantry. This touches your heart deeply because you have been in this situation and know what they are going through at this moment. You try to relate back to your time and feel it. Here, the ignition for empathy comes in. You understand how others feel, and you stop judging people and making assumptions.

Next time when you see that delivery driver delivering food in the rain, your friend taking two jobs to cover his father's medical bill, or the patient who is mentally ill, try to be empathetic. Try to understand what it may be like to be in someone else's shoes. At the end of the day, we need mutual understanding and support.

LEAVE A GOOD LEGACY

We all love to leave the right kind of legacy for our children, community, and world as a whole. The story of a man or woman who succeeded in life, overcoming their adversity, is well remembered. It is even more beautiful when that person helps similar human beings to make the world a better place.

So the biggest and most interesting question you should ask yourself is, "How do I want to be remembered?" Imagine your funeral. If you know someone will be there reflecting on how you overcame your life problems and lived a beautiful life, how you helped and empowered others to build tenacity, you know you are living in such a way that will leave you respected, well honored, and lovingly remembered. Not only does this do justice for your soul, but it also acts as an example to others on how they should lead their lives.

I am happy and grateful if you have taken at least one thing from this little book to advance your life and others'. Yes, sometimes life is unfair and challenging, but grab it with both hands. When life knocks you down, don't accept it. Get up every time, like a Daruma doll.

Pala Wadu Mesthrige

.

.

And

.

.

Go on and paint that "left eye" to chase your hope.
Good luck!

Made in United States
Troutdale, OR
05/09/2025

31213590R00038